Peabody Public Library
Columbia City, IN

J 523.4 BELL
Bell, Trudy E.
The inner planets / Trudy E.
Bell.

NOV 18 08

DISCARD

S0-AGL-139

The Inner Planets

THE NEW SOLAR SYSTEM

TRUDY E. BELL

Peabody Public Library
Columbia City, IN

A⁺

To the middle-schoolers of Messiah Lutheran School, especially my beloved Roxana

—T. E. B.

Published by Smart Apple Media, 1980 Lookout Drive, North Mankato, Minnesota 56003

Copyright © 2003 Byron Preiss Visual Publications
Printed in the United States of America
International copyright reserved in all countries. No part of this book may be reproduced in any form without written permission from the publisher.

Photo Credits: Page 4, 6: courtesy NASA. Page 7: copyright © 2003 William K. Hartmann. Page 8: courtesy NASA. Page 9: copyright © 2003 Calvin J. Hamilton. Page 10: courtesy NASA/ZoomSchool.com. Page 11: NASA/JPL/Northwestern University. Page 13: courtesy NASA. Page 14: courtesy NASA/Calvin J. Hamilton. Page 17: courtesy JET Propulsion Laboratory. Page 18: courtesy NASA/JPL. Page 19, 20: courtesy NASA. Page 21: copyright © 2003 Calvin J. Hamilton. Page 22: copyright © 2003 E. Wolfe, USGS. Page 23: copyright © 2003 Massimo Siragusa. Page 24: copyright © 2003 Calvin J. Hamilton. Page 25, 27: courtesy NASA. Page 28: courtesy Meteor Crater, Northern Arizona, USA. Page 30: courtesy NASA/JPL/Malin Space Sceince Systems. Page 31: courtesy NASA/JPL. Page 32: courtesy NASA. Page 34 (top): courtesy NASA/JPL/Malin Space Science Systems. Page 34 (bottom), 36: courtesy NASA. Page 37: courtesy NASA/JPL/MSSS. Page 38, 39: courtesy NASA. Page 40: courtesy Neelson Crawford/Polar Fine Arts. Page 42: courtesy P. Stomski (W.M. Keck observatory), Caltech, U. California. Page 45: © 2003 Tom Polakis
Cover art courtesy NASA/JPL.

Library of Congress Cataloging-in-Publication Data

Bell, Trudy E.
The inner planets / by Trudy E. Bell.
v. cm. — (The new solar system)
Contents: Origin of the inner planets — Mercury: planet of extremes — Venus: an inferno of a world — The Earth-Moon system: the double planet — Mars: abode of life? — Pleasures of planet-watching. Includes bibliographical references.
ISBN 1-58340-288-8
1. Inner planets—Juvenile literature. [1. Inner planets. 2. Planets] I. Title. II. Series.
QB602.B414 2003   523.4—dc21   2003042514

First Edition

9 8 7 6 5 4 3 2 1

Contents

The inner planets are the four planets nearest the Sun (middle image, which shows the relative sizes of the solar system's planets). Other images are artists' conceptions of the solar system from a distance (not to scale) and the aspects of various planets.

4

Origin of the Inner Planets

How old is our solar system? How did Earth and the other inner planets come into being?

Astronomers still have more questions than answers. They are poring over what they are learning about large, planetlike objects around other stars, meteorites from interplanetary space, and rocks that astronauts have brought back from the Moon. Despite questions about certain details, a general outline does seem clear.

Many observations and samples of interplanetary material suggest that the solar system is almost 4.6 billion—that's 4,600,000,000—years old. Although that seems incredibly old, it's only about a third of the age of the rest of the universe.

Most likely, our solar system began as a vast nebula (cloud of gas and dust), similar to those seen throughout the Milky Way. For many millions of years, the gas and dust swirled aimlessly, until it was disturbed by something—perhaps a shock wave from the explosion of a nearby star. Such a shock wave would have compressed the nebula, causing it to collapse.

As the nebula collapsed, it would have grown hotter and denser in the center. Perhaps in as little as 100,000 years, its center would have heated enough to ignite nuclear "fusion"—a process in which the nuclei of hydrogen atoms combine to form nuclei of helium, releasing vast energy—and thus become a star: the Sun.

Meanwhile, the collapsing nebula would have started to spin faster, just as an ice skater spins faster when she draws her arms close to her body. As it spun faster, the nebula would have flattened into a disk. Particles would have begun to nudge against each other

Peabody Public Library
Columbia City, IN

The four inner planets are also called the "terrestrial" planets, because they are dense and rocky, rather like Earth. Shown here to scale in size (from left to right) are cratered Mercury, volcano-pocked Venus, watery Earth, and desert-parched Mars.

and stick together, gradually growing bigger. Bigger chunks, having greater gravity, would have attracted more particles than smaller ones, growing at the expense of all other nearby objects—eventually becoming planets and satellites.

This early era in the solar system's formation would have been exceptionally violent. Bodies hundreds of miles wide would have slammed into one another and bombarded the growing planets and satellites, gouging huge craters or triggering volcanic activity. Some collisions would have sheared off enormous chunks that might have gone into orbit around planets as moons. Eventually, however, as the growing planets swept up most of the material in the solar nebula, the frequency of catastrophic collisions between truly large bodies would have diminished. But the number of craters on any body in the solar system reveals much about the body's age and past.

How big a planet became depended in large part on its distance from the new Sun and the amount of material in the nebula there. Closer to the new Sun, solar heat would have vaporized ice and frozen gases such as methane and ammonia, leaving behind only denser rocky and metallic materials that coalesced into the "terrestrial" (from the Latin word *terra*, meaning "earth") inner planets: Mercury, Venus, Earth, and Mars. Farther from the new Sun, in the colder outer reaches of the collapsing nebula, icy matter and gases would have condensed, forming the giant gas planets: Jupiter, Saturn, Uranus, and Neptune. Smaller chunks would have formed comets, icy moons, and other objects.

Just because the terrestrial planets formed close to the Sun, however, doesn't mean they are all alike. Far from it! As spacecraft have revealed, each inner planet is its own unique world.

Stars are born of dense nebulae which shrink to form groupings of stars. For the first 50 to 100 million years of the solar system, the Sun and planets were probably embedded in a nebula resembling this artist's conception.

7

This mosaic of images of Mercury from *Mariner 10* (the only spacecraft that has visited Mercury) reveals features as small as a mile (1.6 km) across. Mercury is scarred with impact craters similar to those on the Moon. (The smooth vertical band and isolated smooth patches are regions in which no images were obtained.)

Mercury: Planet of Extremes

Mercury is the second-smallest planet in the solar system after tiny, remote Pluto. In fact, Mercury isn't much bigger than Earth's Moon—only 3,031 miles (4,878 km) in diameter. Yet Mercury's gravity is more than twice that of the Moon because Mercury is the second-densest planet in the solar system, after Earth. Its magnetic field tells us why: Mercury has a large, partly molten iron core nearly three-quarters of its diameter, accounting for 80 percent of its mass. Like Venus, Mercury has no satellite.

The temperature range on Mercury is the most extreme of any planet in the solar system. While temperatures during the day can climb to 800°F (427°C)—hot enough to melt lead—Mercury has almost no atmosphere. (It has an extraordinarily thin atmosphere of hydrogen and helium that actually comes from the Sun, but it's only a

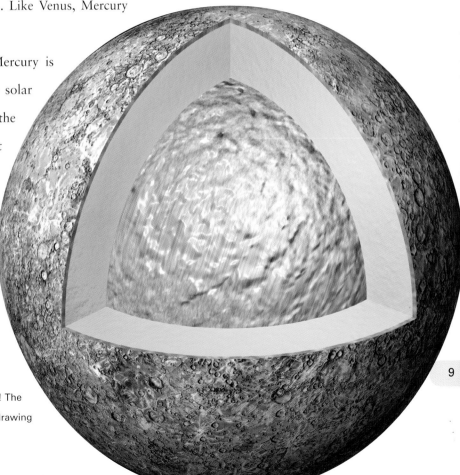

Although Mercury is only a third the size of Earth, its density is almost as great. That indicates that Mercury has a core mostly of iron that is roughly the size of Earth's Moon! The large core is shown in this artist's cutaway drawing of Mercury.

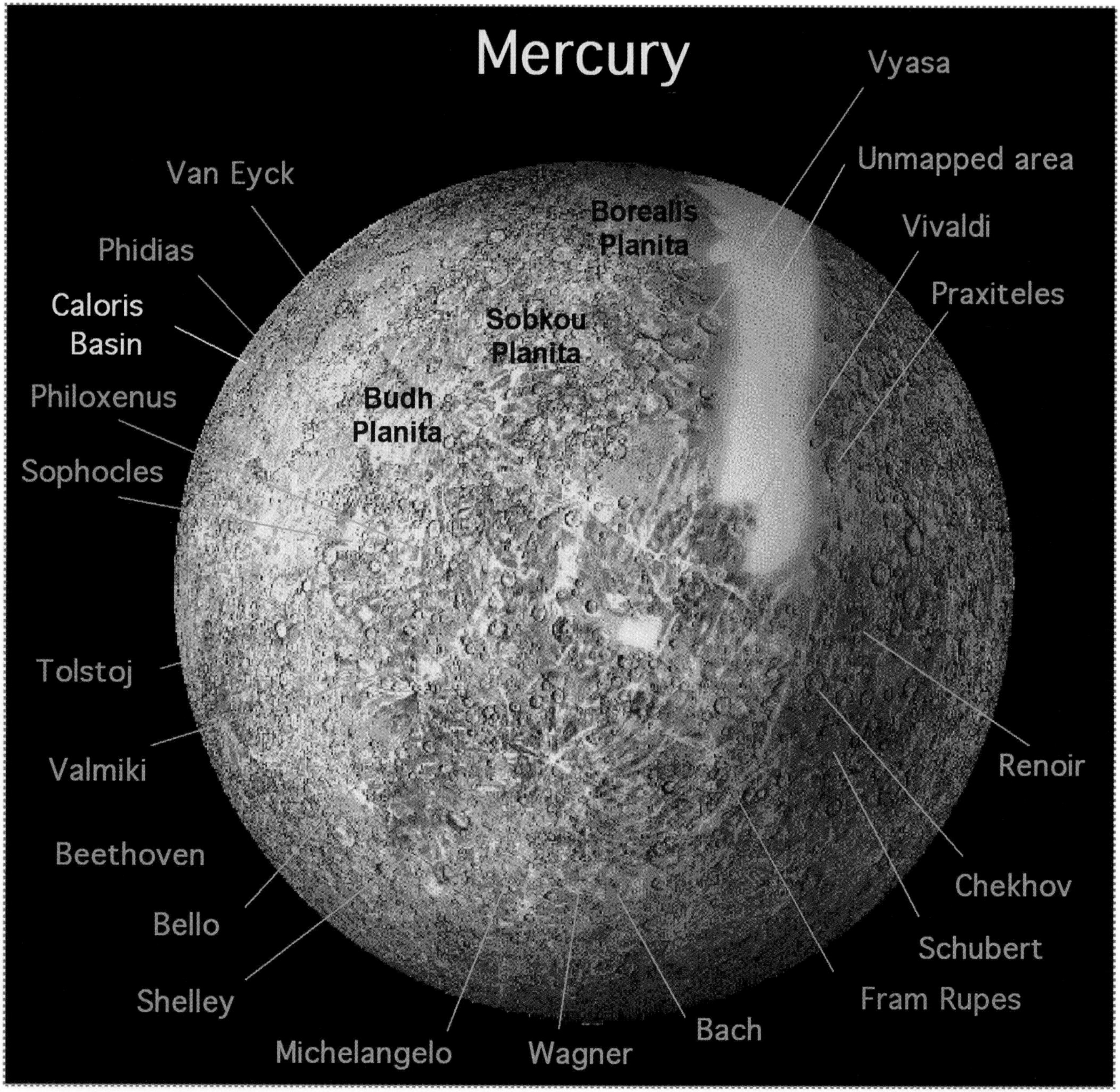

Mercury

Vyasa

Unmapped area

Van Eyck

Vivaldi

Phidias

Borealis
Planita

Praxiteles

Caloris
Basin

Sobkou
Planita

Philoxenus

Budh
Planita

Sophocles

Tolstoj

Renoir

Valmiki

Beethoven

Chekhov

Bello

Schubert

Shelley

Fram Rupes

Michelangelo

Wagner

Bach

The principal surface features of Mercury.

Mercury Mission Highlights

Mercury has been examined close up by just one spacecraft, *Mariner 10*, which made three flybys of Mercury from 1974 to 1975. The probe photographed less than half (45 percent) of its surface, revealing Mercury as a heavily cratered world. It also revealed that Mercury's mass is much greater than previously thought, indicating that Mercury likely has an iron core that makes up 75 percent of the entire planet.

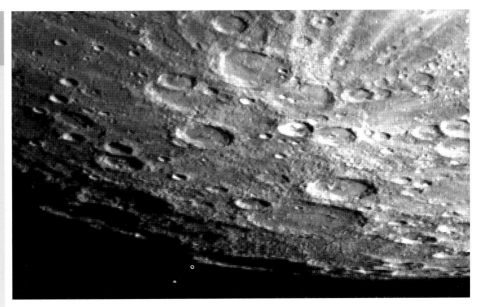

Mercury's south pole was photographed from 53,200 miles (85,800 km) away by *Mariner 10*. The pole itself is located inside the 110-mile (180 km) diameter crater right on the limb (edge) of Mercury (lower center). The bright ray system (upper right) is material splashed out of a 30-mile (50 km) diameter crater.

trillionth as dense as Earth's atmosphere, so it can't act as a thermal blanket.) Therefore, after sunset, temperatures on Mercury rapidly plunge to -270°F (-168°C) and stay there for nearly three Earth months. More remarkably, there are deep craters near both poles where sunlight never reaches the bottom. In these craters, ice actually may exist on this, the closest planet to the Sun. In fact, radar signals from Earth bounced off Mercury's north pole suggest that the ice might even be frozen water, possibly from comets that hit the planet's surface.

Most of what we know about Mercury comes from the *Mariner 10* mission of 1974–1975. Astronomers and planetary geologists keep revisiting these images and data with new computer techniques and new insights from more recent spacecraft visits to other planets.

Mercury's day—as measured from sunrise to sunrise, as we think of a day on Earth—is twice as long as its year. In other words, every Mercurian day, you'd celebrate your Mercurian birthday twice!

How can that be?

Mercury's orbit is the smallest of all the planets: Mercury's year—the time it takes to revolve once around the Sun—is thus the shortest: 88 Earth days, or just less than three Earth months. Although Mercury spins once on its axis to face the same stars in 59 days—its sidereal day—in that same time the planet has proceeded two-thirds of the way around its orbit. Thus the Sun is in a completely different part of the sky. Indeed, it takes Mercury 176 Earth days to rotate once and face the Sun—Mercury's solar day. That means Mercury's solar day is two full Mercurian years, or three sidereal days, long! (On Earth the two types of days are almost the same—24 hours for the solar day versus 23 hours and 56 minutes for the sidereal day. The only effect of their four-minute difference is to make the nighttime constellations slowly migrate across the sky throughout the year as Earth orbits the Sun.)

Also, from Mercury's surface, the Sun would appear to swell and shrink! Mercury's orbit is not a perfect circle like Earth's. Instead, it's elliptical (egg-shaped), meaning that sometimes Mercury is less than a third of Earth's distance from the Sun (less than 29 million miles or 47 million km), and sometimes it is nearly half of Earth's distance from the sun (more than 43 million miles or 70 million km). So, from Mercury's surface over the course of each Mercurian year, the Sun would slowly appear to swell up in the sky until it was three times the diameter it appears from Earth, and then slowly shrink again until it was twice the diameter!

As if that weren't weird enough, the Sun would also do a strange dance in the sky. Mercury dramatically speeds up and slows down along its elliptical orbit as it approaches and recedes from the Sun. Thus, each Mercurian solar day, the Sun would appear to stop in the sky, reverse course for a little ways, then resume its forward movement again!

Superficially, Mercury's surface resembles that of the Moon. Mercury is pocked with thousands of impact craters, resembling the ancient lunar highlands. It also is covered with smooth lava flows in large, relatively flat plains called "*planitia*" (plah-NEE-chee-ah) reminiscent of the lunar "*maria*" (Latin for "seas"), although the *maria* on the Moon are darker than the *planitia* on Mercury. Did the lava come from erupting volcanoes, as on the Moon? Or was it liquefied material ejected from basins after an immense impact from an exceptionally large object? Recent analysis suggests that at least some of its smooth plains are likely volcanic; the relative lack of craters on the *planitia* also suggest they are recent.

There are also important differences between Mercury and the Moon. For example, Mercury's surface is crisscrossed with long mountainous escarpments, or cliffs. Towering up to a mile (1.6 km) high, these scarps heaved up when Mercury slightly

contracted some four billion years ago, causing Mercury's crust to crack as it cooled and shrank.

One of the largest features on Mercury is the Caloris Basin, more than 800 miles (1,300 km) in diameter. Its concentric rings of mountains, as well as the jumbled terrain on the planet's opposite hemisphere, suggests that the basin resulted from the violent impact of an asteroid more than 60 miles (100 km) in diameter early in the planet's history.

The largest feature on Mercury is the Caloris Basin (the large half- circular feature at the right), which is 800 miles (1,300 km) across. The Caloris Basin, which gets very hot as it is the point directly under the Sun when Mercury is closest to the Sun, is likely the result of an asteroid hit.

13

Just how cloudy is Venus? It's virtually featureless at visible wavelengths. This photograph was taken from the *Galileo* spacecraft in 1990, as it swung past Venus on its way to Jupiter. Venus's unbroken, thick clouds trap heat, making it the hottest planet in the solar system.

Venus: An Inferno of a World

From Earth, Venus's dazzling brilliance as the evening or morning star inspired the ancient Greeks and Romans to name it after their goddess of love and beauty. Venus is so close in size to Earth as almost to be Earth's twin—inspiring early 20th-century science-fiction writers to imagine its surface teeming with prehistoric jungle life, warmed by being closer to the Sun. But the harsh reality, revealed by numerous United States and Russian spacecraft, dashed such romantic fantasies.

Although the cream-colored sphere of clouds appears almost featureless by reflected visible sunlight, surveys taken at wavelengths shorter than visible light cut through the cloud layers to reveal that the planet is belted with huge, dark, C-shaped and sideways Y-shaped striations that form, swirl, and dissolve. They reveal that high-speed winds in the upper atmosphere are rushing at nearly 200 miles (300 km) per hour, circling the whole planet in four days. Planetary meteorologists are still trying to understand this rapid pattern of what they call "superrotation."

Despite the high-speed winds aloft, at the surface, the soupy atmosphere barely stirs at two or three miles (3–5 km) per hour. The movement is more like a deep-ocean current than like a faint breeze, as the surface pressure on Venus is 92 times the atmospheric pressure at sea level on Earth! That's equivalent to the pressure found 0.6 mile (1 km) deep in Earth's oceans and is higher even than the pressure inside the space shuttle's solid rocket boosters at ignition. To humans, the Venusian air would be noxious. It is 95 percent carbon dioxide (the waste gas mammals exhale), the rest being mostly nitrogen, with virtually no free oxygen. And the thick Venusian clouds are composed of droplets of sulfuric acid—essentially pure battery acid: one of the most corrosive and poisonous acids known, which can dissolve many metals as well as living tissue.

Moreover, Venus is the hottest planet in the solar system. Night and day, the surface temperature hovers at nearly 900°F (480°C). Not only is that hotter than the melting point of aluminum and other spacecraft materials and electronics, it's even hotter than midday on Mercury! How can Venus be hotter than Mercury when it's twice as far from the Sun? Think of a car with its windows rolled up parked outside on a sunny day; the window glass allows in visible sunlight that heats the interior of the car, but almost completely blocks longer-wavelength infrared light (heat radiation) from getting back out. The heat is trapped inside, adding to the energy from the incoming sunlight and heating the car's interior like a solar oven. That effect—the greenhouse effect—is well known to gardeners who rely on it to grow tomatoes in greenhouses in midwinter. On Venus, even below 40 miles (66 km) of clouds, enough sunlight filters through so that the surface is as bright as a heavily overcast day on Earth. That sunlight bakes the dry rocks that spacecraft landers have seen scattered around on Venus's surface. The warm rocks reradiate heat, but the planet's thick carbon dioxide atmosphere blocks the heat from escaping back into space. The heat trapped in the atmosphere makes Venus extremely hot.

Within about an hour, the combination of blistering heat, crushing pressure, and caustic clouds have destroyed the electronics in all spacecraft that have landed on Venus. Nonetheless, although our eyes can't see through Venus's thick clouds in visible light, radio waves penetrate them easily, bouncing off the planet's surface and back up to spacecraft in orbit. Thus, spacecraft imaging systems viewing the planet at radio wavelengths have mapped Venus's surface in great detail.

Venus Mission Highlights

Venus has been explored by spacecraft more than 20 times. *Mariner 2* (1962) and *Mariner 5* (1967) discovered Venus's scorching temperature and crushing atmospheric pressure. The Soviet spacecraft *Venera 9* (1975) was the first to soft-land on Venus's surface and return black-and-white photographs of the rocky desert landscape (before its electronics were fried by the hostile conditions), followed by the first color pictures by *Venera 13* (1982). Several NASA spacecraft—notably *Magellan* (1990–1994)—have mapped Venus's surface in great detail from orbit 150 to 250 miles (240–400 km) above the planet, using radar to see beneath the thick clouds. *Magellan* found that volcanoes have shaped 85 percent of Venus with lava plains, lava domes, large shield volcanoes, and extremely long lava channels.

This three-dimensional perspective view of the surface of
Venus reveals circular, volcanic domelike hills. The average
diameter of each hill is 15 miles (25 km), with an altitude of
up to 2,500 feet (750 m). The bright margins of the hills may
indicate rock debris at the base of their slopes. This image was
synthesized from data from three spacecraft (*Magellan* and
Venera 13 and *14*).

The five-mile (8 km) high volcano *Maat Mons* on Venus is surrounded by lava flows for hundreds of miles in this three-dimensional image synthesized from data from three spacecraft (*Magellan* and *Venera 13* and *14*). *Mons* means "mountain" in Latin, and *Maat* was the Egyptian goddess of truth and justice.

Strange Venus Sun Tricks

Until the first radar signals from Earth bounced off the surface of Venus in 1961, astronomers had no inkling about the length of Venus's day. And what a surprise the radar revealed. Instead of rotating once in about 24 hours, as does Earth, Venus's sidereal day is 243 Earth days long. Because Venus's year is only 225 Earth days (about 7 Earth months) long, that makes its sidereal day longer than its year.

Moreover, Venus rotates "retrograde"—that is, in the opposite direction of its orbital rotation. In other words, as seen from its north pole, Venus rotates clockwise, instead of counterclockwise, as is the case with Earth and all other planets and satellites except Uranus and Pluto.

The ultimate effect of the Venusian year being shorter than the Venusian sidereal day, plus the planet's retrograde rotation, is that Venus's solar day (from one sunrise to the next, as we think of a day on Earth) is 117 Earth days long. Moreover, the Sun—to the extent that it could be seen as a brighter spot behind the thick clouds—would appear to rise in the west and set in the east!

And what is there? Volcanoes, volcanoes, and still more volcanoes! Because oceanless Venus is bone dry, it has three times the land area of Earth; and a good 90 percent of it is covered with volcanoes. Vast, low-lying flat flows of lava resemble the dark, smooth lunar maria. The lava flows are dotted with thousands of shield volcanoes that are relatively small—less than 12 miles (19 km) across—that crop up in clusters, similar to clusters of shield volcanoes that dot Earth's ocean floors. Intriguingly, however, some of the lava flows look as fresh as if they had erupted yesterday. Although planetary geologists haven't yet seen a Venusian volcano spewing lava, evidence is strong that they're still active, just as they are on Earth.

Most of the craters on Venus seem to be of volcanic, rather than impact, origin. In fact, compared to other planets, Venus displays the fewest number of impact craters, none smaller than two miles (3 km) in diameter. Those that do exist seem remarkably unweathered. From this evidence, planetary geologists suspect all of Venus may have been resurfaced—covered with fresh lava—as recently as 300 to 500 million years ago (although they continue to debate how and why). Since then, most incoming projectiles most likely have been small enough to break up and vaporize in Venus's thick atmosphere, never making it to the surface.

Planetary Radius (km)

6048 6050 6052 6054 6056 6058 6060 6062

This color-coded relief map of Venus's surface was made by combining data from *Magellan*'s radar altimeter (altitude-measuring instrument) with a mosaic of imaging-radar images. Purples and blues represent the lowest surfaces, followed by greens, yellows, and oranges, with reds representing the highest points.

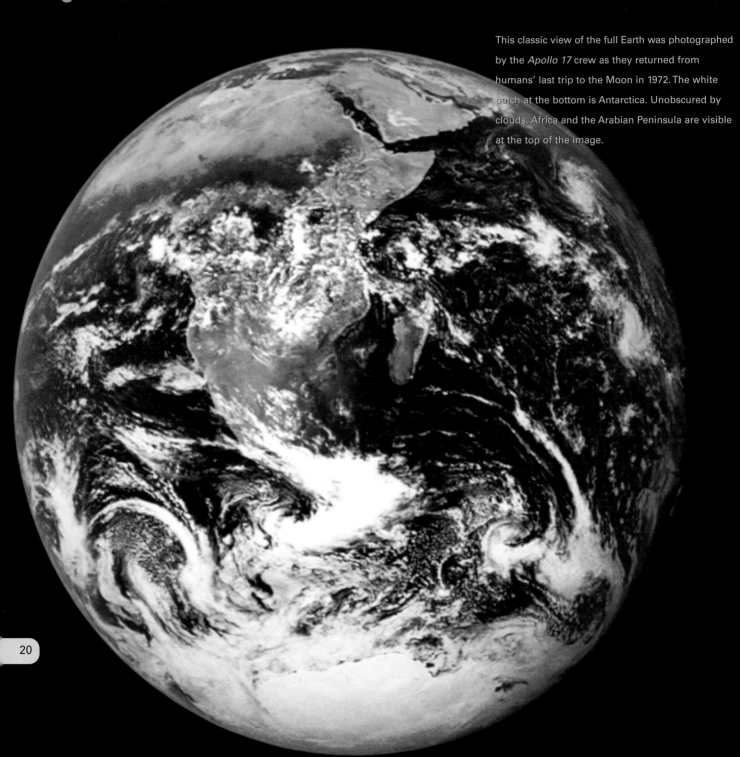

This classic view of the full Earth was photographed by the *Apollo 17* crew as they returned from humans' last trip to the Moon in 1972. The white patch at the bottom is Antarctica. Unobscured by clouds, Africa and the Arabian Peninsula are visible at the top of the image.

CHAPTER THREE

The Earth-Moon System:
The Double Planet

Of all the terrestrial planets, Earth is the largest and densest. At its center is a solid core of nickel and iron, where the temperature is actually hotter than on the surface of the Sun—nearly 13,000°F (7,000°C)! Above the core is a hot, semifluid mantle, composed primarily of molten rock. And encircling all of this is Earth's relatively thin crust.

The crust is not one solid piece: It actually consists of eight major solid plates (plus 20 or more smaller plates), all floating in constant motion on the hot mantle. Where one plate grinds past or dives beneath another (a process called "subduction") earthquakes rumble, mountain ranges heave up, and magma wells up into volcanoes and spews out as molten lava. Where two plates drift apart (a process called "spreading"), magma wells up and forms new crust. So, although Earth is the same age as the rest of the solar system, its crust is constantly being created and destroyed. Rare is the rock that is older than about three billion years, and most are much younger.

This artist's cutaway view of Earth shows that its crust is about 20 miles (30 km) thick. It floats on the molten mantle, which is about 1,700 miles (2,800 km) thick. In the center is a core of mostly iron about 2,100 miles (3,500 km) in radius—larger than the Moon.

21

Earth is volcanically active. The Kupaianaha lava pond in Hawaii formed in 1986 as a vent named Kupaianaha in the active volcano Kilauea steadily poured out lava for more than five years. Cracks zigzagging across the thin crust of the black lava reveal the red-hot molten rock below. The circular part of the pond is about 110 yards (100 m) in diameter.

Like the other planets in the solar system, Earth was heavily bombarded early in its history. Some ancient impact craters are still visible on its surface, although most are heavily eroded by wind and weather. Geologists believe they have even identified the crater in the Yucatan Peninsula of Mexico formed by the collision that may have caused the extinction of the dinosaurs!

What makes Earth unique, however, is that it's the only planet at the right distance from the Sun and with an atmosphere thick enough so that water can remain liquid on its surface. Mars's water is ice beneath its surface; water on the other inner planets has long since vaporized or exists only in trace amounts as frost. But liquid water on Earth abounds, raining from the sky into cascading waterfalls and vast oceans and evaporating again into clouds—the perpetual and life-sustaining water cycle.

For that, we have the greenhouse effect to thank. Yes, the same effect that has turned Venus into a parched inferno has made

One of the biggest and most famous active volcanoes on Earth is the 10,900-foot (3,300 meter) high Mount Etna in Sicily, Italy. On July 17, 2001, it began erupting in its most violent outburst in 10 years; this particular photograph was taken at night on July 25. Other places where volcanoes erupt frequently include Hawaii and Iceland.

Earth Mission Highlights

Earth has been explored from space since the 1960s by scores of satellites, as well as by special-purpose instruments carried aboard aircraft and the space shuttle. Missions have included tracking ocean currents, exploring for minerals, monitoring Arctic and Antarctic ice packs, observing the health of forests and farm fields, tracing the effects of earthquakes and other natural disasters, and radar-mapping regions of the Amazonian jungle perpetually shrouded by clouds.

This artist's cutaway drawing shows the lunar crust is thicker than Earth's. It ranges from tens of miles under mare basins to more than 60 miles (100 km) in some highland regions. It, too, floats on a molten mantle. The tiny core, possibly made of mostly iron, is only 200 to 250 miles (300–425 km) in radius.

life possible on Earth. Earth's atmosphere is 77 percent nitrogen and 21 percent oxygen, but traces of carbon dioxide act as the window glass in that car in the sunny parking lot. On Earth, the greenhouse effect has raised the average surface temperature from a frigid -6°F (-21°C) to a comfortable 57°F (14°C); without it, the oceans would freeze and life as we know it would be impossible.

There is as much carbon dioxide on Earth as there is on Venus; it's just not all in the atmosphere. Instead, Earth's carbon dioxide has been integrated in solid form in carbonate rocks. Carbon dioxide can be written as a chemical component as follows: CO_2. Limestone is a type of rock that is essentially a calcium carbonate ($CaCO_3$). Other carbonate rocks may contain magnesium, iron, and other minerals instead of calcium. If such rocks are heated enough, the carbonate burns off as carbon dioxide, as it has on Venus, to form the CO_2 atmosphere. To a lesser extent, Earth's remaining carbon dioxide has dissolved in the oceans and is consumed by living plants.

But that's a delicate balance. Burning fossil fuels such as coal and oil in automobiles and in electric-power plants belches far more carbon dioxide into the atmosphere than is exhaled by all the animals on Earth. At the same time, humans all over Earth are cutting down

Moon Mission Highlights

The Moon has been visited more than three dozen times by Soviet or U.S. spacecraft that have crashed into the lunar surface, orbited the Moon, or soft-landed on it. Most notable were the six manned *Apollo* missions (*Apollo 11*, *12*, *14*, *15*, *16*, and *17*) that landed between 1969 and 1972, during which astronauts explored different regions of the moon by rover and by foot and returned to Earth with 842 pounds (382 kg) of lunar rocks.

On July 20, 1969, *Apollo 11* astronauts were the first humans to set foot on another heavenly body—Earth's Moon. Here Neil A. Armstrong (left) and Edwin E. "Buzz" Aldrin Jr. (right) set up a U.S. flag in the *Mare Tranquilitatis* (the Sea of Tranquillity).

the trees and vegetation that absorb our waste carbon dioxide and generate life-giving oxygen through photosynthesis. Will a net excess of industrial carbon dioxide mean a runaway greenhouse effect that will forever alter Earth's climate, as some environmentalists fear? Only time will tell.

Earth has a natural satellite that is so large it is sometimes classified as a planet itself: the Moon. The Moon is also the only extraterrestrial body to have been visited by humans. *Apollo* astronauts visited between 1969 and 1972 six times, and returned to Earth with 842 pounds (382 kg) of lunar rocks.

At 2,140 miles (3,420 km) across, the Moon is more than a quarter of Earth's size. But it has only 60 percent of the density of Earth, so its gravity is only 17 percent that of Earth. The Moon's gravity is so weak that it cannot hang onto an atmosphere.

The Moon consists of two basic types of terrain. The first is large, smooth, dark areas called lunar *maria* (Latin plural for "seas"; singular is *mare*), because early astronomers speculated they might be vast oceans. The *maria* cover about 16 percent of the Moon's surface. We now know that *maria* are vast, low-lying plains of lava ranging from 120 to 720 miles (200–1,200 km) across. Based on the Moon rocks the *Apollo* astronauts brought to Earth, geologists have dated the youngest *maria* as a billion years old!

The other significant type of lunar terrain is heavily cratered lunar highlands. Analyses of lunar rocks have revealed the highlands to be some of the most ancient terrain in the solar system. Their chemistry is very similar to Earth rocks, but they are far older, dating back between 3 and 4.6 billion years to the solar system's earliest days. From studying them, most scientists now believe the Moon formed when a Mars-sized object slammed into Earth 60 million years after Earth formed. The ejected material then coalesced into the Moon.

Most of the Moon's surface is also coated with regolith, talcum-fine dust and rocky debris formed over billions of years by the high-speed impacts of microscopic meteorites eroding the rocks. Before the first unmanned *Surveyor* spacecraft soft-landed on the moon and found the dust to be shallow,

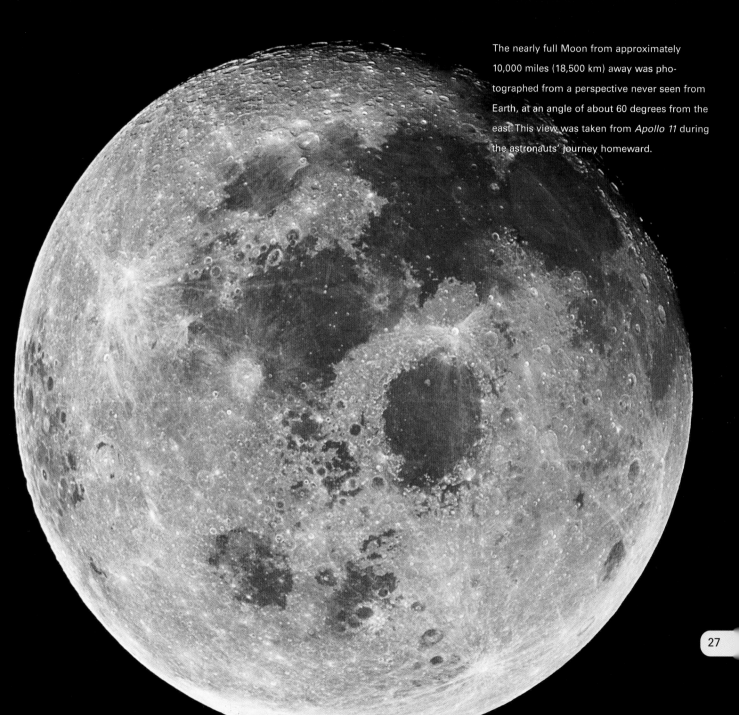

The nearly full Moon from approximately 10,000 miles (18,500 km) away was photographed from a perspective never seen from Earth, at an angle of about 60 degrees from the east. This view was taken from *Apollo 11* during the astronauts' journey homeward.

astronomers feared the Moon might be thickly blanketed with dust (the premise of a famous early science-fiction novel by Arthur C. Clarke called *A Fall of Moon Dust*).

The Moon is so big and so close to Earth—only 230,000 miles (384,000 km) away—that its gravitational attraction exerts significant effects on Earth. Most significantly, the Moon causes the water in the oceans, large bodies of fresh water such as the Great Lakes, and even dry land to bulge out toward the Moon. As Earth rotates under this gravitational pull, the bulge moves around Earth once a day, causing tides.

Earth's stronger gravity exerts an even more powerful effect on the Moon, causing it to keep one hemisphere more or less facing Earth. Moreover, the tidal interaction is slowing the Earth's rotation by about 1.5 milliseconds per century, which is causing the Moon to spiral away from the Earth at about 2.5 inches (4 cm) per year. That doesn't sound like much, but evidence suggests that 900 million years ago, an Earth year might have consisted of 481 eighteen-hour days!

Earth bears the scars of past impacts from meteorites and asteroids. One of the freshest is the Barringer Meteor Crater outside Flagstaff, Arizona, believed to be less than 50,000 years old. The crater is more than 0.6 mile (1 km) in diameter. Today more than 100 impact craters have been identified on Earth.

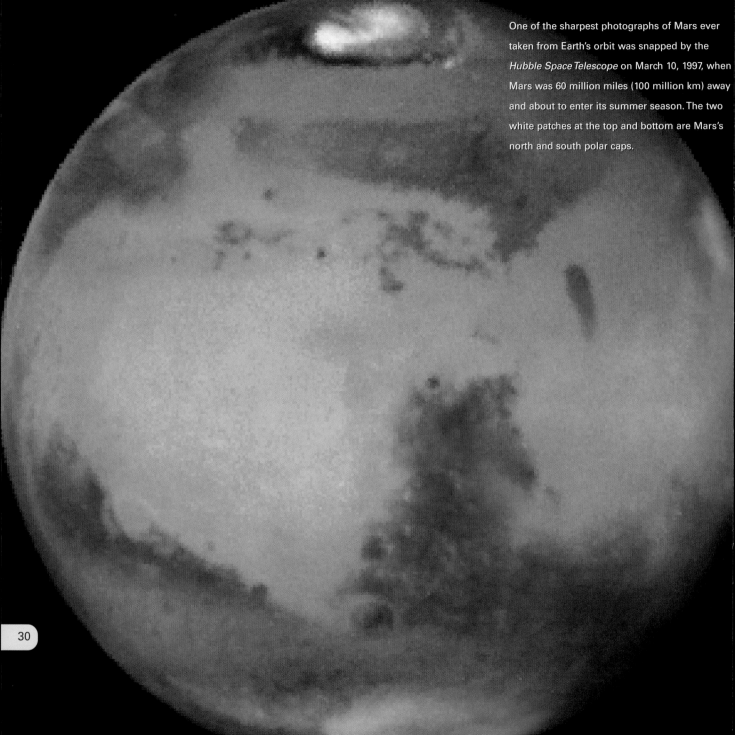

One of the sharpest photographs of Mars ever taken from Earth's orbit was snapped by the *Hubble Space Telescope* on March 10, 1997, when Mars was 60 million miles (100 million km) away and about to enter its summer season. The two white patches at the top and bottom are Mars's north and south polar caps.

Even from Earth, it is obvious why Mars has been dubbed the red planet: It gleams red in the starry sky, its bloody color inspiring the ancient Romans to name it after their god of war. Orbiting and landing spacecraft have revealed that, up close, the landscape ranges from deep brown to terra cotta red, the color of bricks or clay flowerpots. Those reddish soils are rich in iron oxides—compounds similar to the reddish rust that forms on a steel bicycle left out in the rain.

This panoramic view of the surface of Mars was taken by the *Pathfinder* lander. Approximately 100 photograph frames have been compiled to produce this single, seamless image.

Of all the planets in the solar system, Mars has fascinated scientists and science-fiction writers the most, because of "the big question": Is there life on Mars?

From ground-based telescopes, astronomers could—and still can—watch Mars change with the seasons; its polar ice caps shrink in Martian spring and summer, and equatorial regions darken as if vegetation were growing. Even at one-and-a-half times as far from the Sun as Earth, astronomers thought Mars would be chilly but perhaps not colder than the Arctic, where people and animals have lived for millennia. Although Mars's winter lows can reach -220°F (-140°C)—significantly colder than any low ever recorded in Siberia or Antarctica—Martian summers can hit a balmy 68°F (20°C).

What would human travelers find on Mars?
This is one artist's speculation about what
astronauts might encounter.

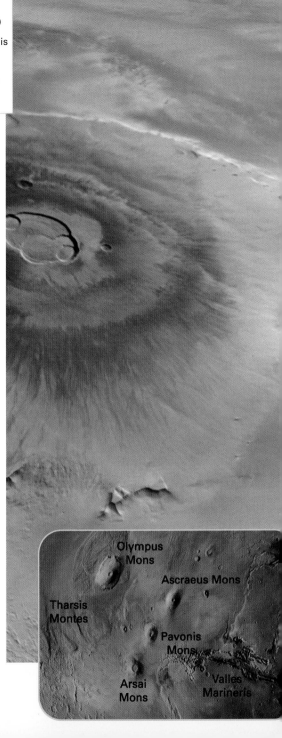

Olympus Mons (Mount Olympus) is the largest volcano in the solar system. It is 350 miles (600 km) in diameter and stands 15 miles (24 km) above the surrounding plains—three times as high as Mount Everest. It is a shield volcano, the same type that formed the Hawaiian Islands on Earth and that are also seen on Venus. The inset map shows three other major Martian volcanoes and part of *Valles Marineris*.

Olympus Mons

Ascraeus Mons

Tharsis Montes

Pavonis Mons

Arsai Mons

Valles Marineris

At 4,222 miles (6,794 km) in diameter, Mars is twice the size of the Moon, with more than twice its gravity (38 percent of the gravity of Earth). That's big enough to retain an atmosphere. Mars's atmosphere is not breathable to humans, as it's 95 percent carbon dioxide, with the rest being mostly nitrogen and argon (there's almost no oxygen). It's only a hundredth as thick as Earth's atmosphere but thick enough to be seen from orbiting spacecraft as a thin haze clinging to the distant horizon. Most importantly, though, the atmosphere is thick enough to have occasional clouds and fog—signs of water vapor. And where there's water, perhaps there's life—so reasoned astronomers and science-fiction novelists well into the 20th century. These hopes partially motivated the earliest space-craft missions to Mars.

Although spacecraft missions in the 1960s and 1970s revealed that Mars is a desert planet, dry river beds and unmistakable signs of liquid erosion testified to a past abundant with flowing surface water. Photos of layered terrain taken by the *Mars Global Surveyor* in 2000 even suggest there may have been large lakes or even small oceans some 4 billion years ago.

Other observations powerfully suggest that water still

abounds on Mars, mostly as ice. For example, detailed measurements of the heights of the polar ice caps revealed them to be two to three miles (3–5 km) high in the depths of winter. The topmost layers are undoubtedly dry ice, or frozen carbon dioxide—the same material butchers use for packing and shipping frozen meats. But now planetary geologists believe the ice caps' supporting layers must be water ice, because dry ice simply isn't structurally strong enough to stand miles high. In 2002, the *Mars Odyssey* spacecraft further rekindled hopes of the existence of abundant water ice by discovering huge deposits of hydrogen just under Mars's surface, most likely in the form of ice-impregnated soils. The volume of ice is so great that if it were melted, the resulting water would be double the volume of Lake Michigan.

Even more exciting are *Mars Global Surveyor*'s high-resolution photographs of thousands of fine networks of branching gullies, especially on the shaded side of small hills facing the polar ice caps. These gullies strongly resemble washes in Earth's deserts that occur after flash floods, even down to the fan-shaped pile of debris left near the bottom of the rise where the flow died. Some gullies look so fresh they are clearly very recent—perhaps only centuries, years, or even just weeks old! The gullies suggest that swimming-pool volumes of liquid water might have been entombed underground; subterranean warming allows the water to gush up to the surface and pour down the slopes. Alternately, the

Mars Mission Highlights

Mars has been visited by more than a dozen U.S. and Soviet spacecraft since 1965. Notable among them were the *Viking 1* and *2* landers (1976), which chemically analyzed Martian soil for microorganisms (there is still debate as to whether the probes found life there or not) and sent back color panoramas of their surroundings during various seasons. Also notable was *Mars Global Surveyor* (1997), which orbited Mars for more than three full Martian years (more than five Earth years), returning more data about the red planet than all other Mars missions combined. Among its key findings are high-resolution pictures of gullies and debris flow features that suggest there may be current sources of liquid water, similar to an aquifer, at or near the surface of the planet. Its findings were corroborated by *Odyssey*, which went into orbit around Mars in 2001 to map elements and minerals, look for evidence of water, and study the radiation environment. In 2002, it discovered evidence of what is believed to be large concentrations of frozen water in the Martian soil just below the surface across much of the planet.

35

Ice-rich layers of Martian soils were detected by instruments aboard NASA's *Mars Odyssey* in 2001. The instruments detected the signature of hydrogen, indicating water ice about three feet (1 m) under the surface; their total depth is unknown. This artist's rendering is not to scale, as the spacecraft was orbiting at an altitude of 250 miles (400 km).

gullies might be places where snow melt has run off down slopes.

While there is still uncertainty about life on Mars, there is no question that Martian geology is dramatic. Some features on Mars are so magnificently huge that they can be appreciated only from orbit. One is a crevasse that makes Earth's Grand Canyon look puny. *Valles Marineris* (VAL-less mair-I-NAIR-ess, Latin for "Mariner Valley") is the grandest canyon in the entire solar system. Ten times as long as the Grand Canyon, it is the width of the United States and a fifth the circumference of Mars! Stretching 2,500 miles (4,000 km) long, it's as deep as 4 miles (7 km) and as wide as 125 miles (200 km) in some places. Scientists believe it's a huge crack in Mars's crust that formed as the planet cooled.

Mars is also home to *Olympus Mons* (Latin for "Mount Olympus," the home of the gods in Greek mythology). This monumental name describes a monumental feature, as *Olympus Mons* is the biggest shield volcano in the entire solar system. At about

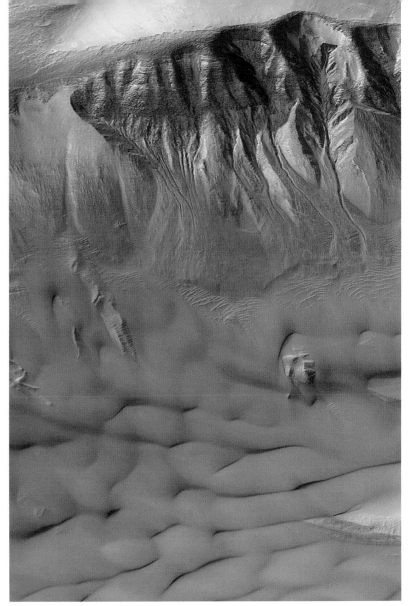

Small gullies, such as these carved into the side of the Noachis impact crater, suggest liquid water might exist just below the Martian surface. Found at middle and high latitudes, especially in Mars's southern hemisphere, the gullies appear to be evidence of recent groundwater seepage and surface runoff or perhaps melting from snow packs.

350 miles (600 km) across, it is wider than the state of New Mexico; at 15 miles (24 km) high, it stands three times as high as Mount Everest. Its caldera (the central crater from which all the lava flowed) itself is 50 miles (80 km) across, big enough to cradle all of the greater Los Angeles area. *Olympus Mons* and many other shield volcanoes on Mars tell us volcanic activity was crucial in shaping the planet.

Mars possesses two very small moons believed to be captured asteroids. The larger one is cratered, potato-shaped Phobos, less than 14 miles (22 km) in diameter and in an orbit only 5,400 miles (9,000 km) above Mars. It's so close, in fact, that it zips around the planet three times a day! The smaller one is Deimos, which is only about half that size and nearly three times as distant.

Valles Marineris (Mariner Valley) is the grandest canyon in the solar system, running 2,500 miles (4,000 km)—the width of the entire United States—along the Martian equator, at places reaching 4 miles (7 km) deep. By comparison, the Grand Canyon in Arizona is 500 miles (800 km) long and 1 mile (1.6 km) deep. Unlike the Grand Canyon, which was formed by erosion from the Colorado River, Valles Marineris is likely a tectonic "crack" in the Martian crust that formed as the planet cooled.

This image of Phobos, the inner and larger of the two moons of Mars, was taken by the *Mars Global Surveyor* on August 19, 1998. The minimum distance between the spacecraft and Phobos was 671 miles (1,080 km). This image is one of the highest resolution images ever obtained of the Martian satellite.

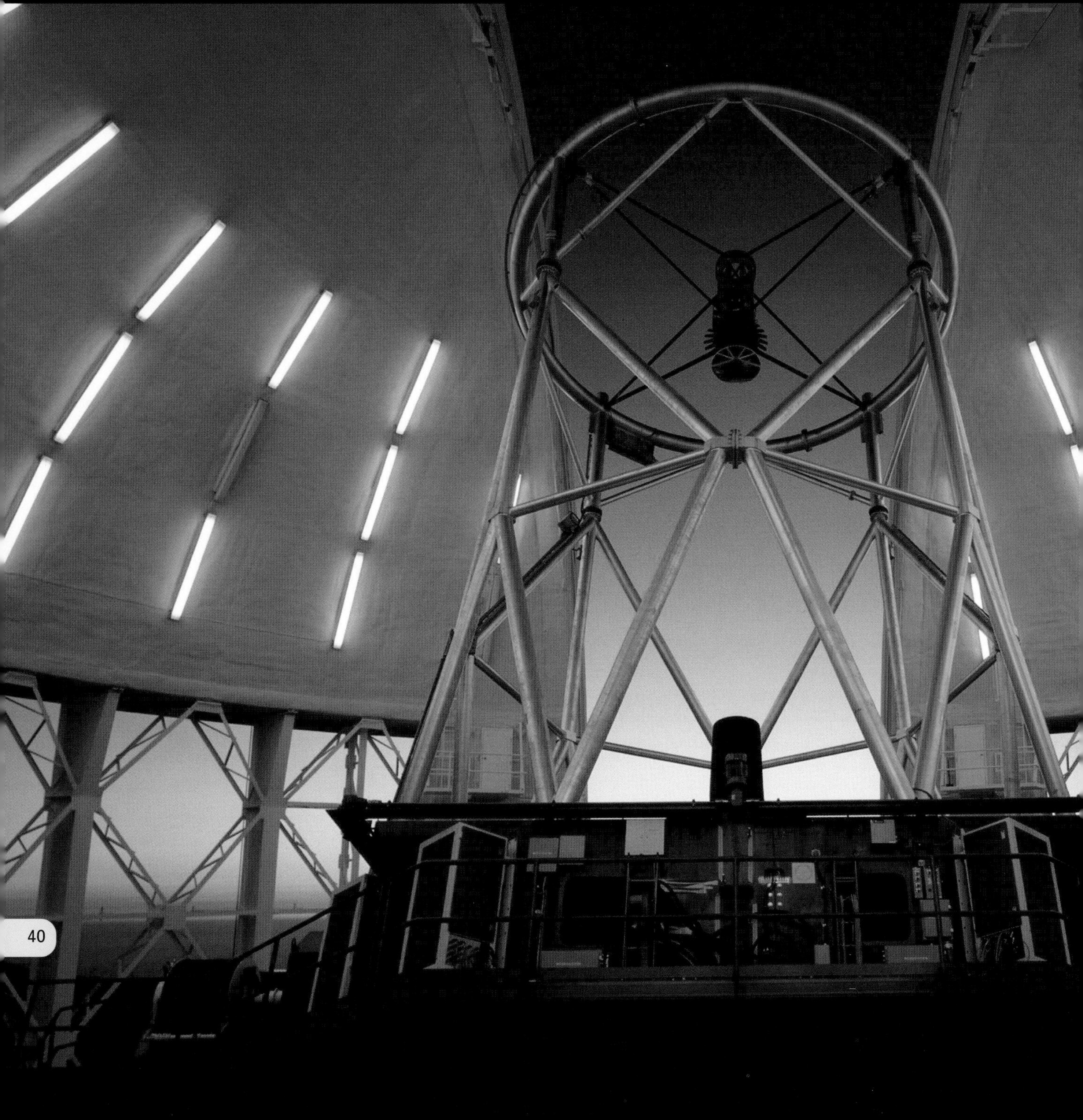

"Starlight, star bright, first star I see tonight…" is probably a planet. Scanning the skies at dusk, one can first make educated guesses about what is showing, and then confirm the observation by checking a daily newspaper, monthly astronomy magazine, or Web site. Many list the times of sunset and sunrise as well as the phases of the Moon and which planets are visible.

The very first and brightest star seen in the west around sunset as "the evening star," or in the east around sunrise as "the morning star," is likely the planet Venus. If looking at it through a pair of binoculars, one would see a miniature crescent, appearing just like a tiny Moon. Indeed, Venus goes through phases just like the Moon, which can be seen by looking at it every night for a month or two. Venus's phases, in fact, convinced Italian scientist Galileo Galilei centuries ago that Venus revolves around the Sun and not around the Earth.

A fainter starlike object still lower in the sky is almost lost in the glare of twilight. If in binoculars it also appears as a crescent, then it is Mercury, the planet of extremes.

DISCARD

Sunset peeks through vents in the walls of Gemini North, an observatory housing a telescope atop Mauna Kea, Hawaii, having a mirror more than 26 feet (8.1 m) across. An identical twin observatory, Gemini South, is atop Chile's Cerro Pachón. The dry air and high altitude of both sites allow the two telescopes to obtain some of the sharpest images of astronomical objects from anywhere on Earth, rivaling even the *Hubble Space Telescope* in orbit.

41

When night has fallen completely, an object whose steady reddish gleam looks noticeably different from the twinkling points of the stars may appear. That would be Mars. If its surface markings are studied through a small telescope over several months, its polar icecaps can be seen to grow and shrink with its seasons.

Even with unaided eyes, one can learn how the Moon and inner planets move in the solar system. Get a star map, or draw one of what is visible overhead. Tonight, note the phase of the Moon and its position with respect to background constellations. Tomorrow night, see how dra-

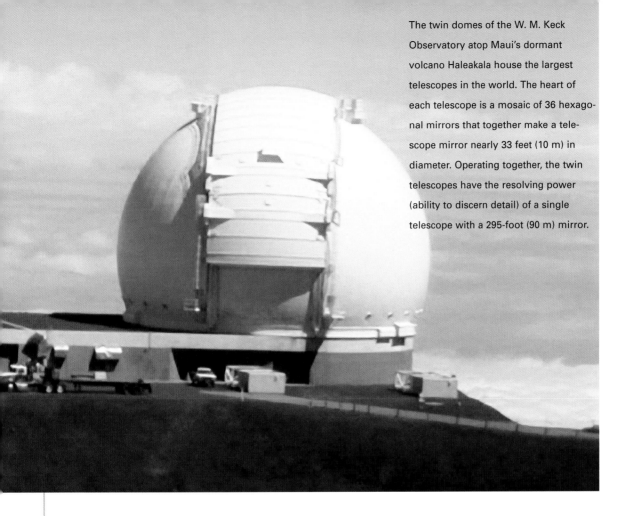

The twin domes of the W. M. Keck Observatory atop Maui's dormant volcano Haleakala house the largest telescopes in the world. The heart of each telescope is a mosaic of 36 hexagonal mirrors that together make a telescope mirror nearly 33 feet (10 m) in diameter. Operating together, the twin telescopes have the resolving power (ability to discern detail) of a single telescope with a 295-foot (90 m) mirror.

matically both its phase and position have changed. Update the chart every clear night for the next month. (Warning: To follow the Moon for an entire orbit, an alarm will need to be set for the middle of the night for nearly two weeks!) How long will it take the Moon to return to the first place it first appeared against the background of stars (its sidereal period)?

Also tonight, plot where Mercury, Venus, and Mars appear. Do the same thing tomorrow night—and then the next night, and the next. Within a week or two, even with a homemade map, it will be clear how the planets wander through the stars—why the ancient Greeks knew they were somehow different from the fixed stars and named them planets, or wanderers. Keep observing them faithfully over the next year or two, and eventually they will disappear behind the Sun and reappear in the morning sky.

Want to impress people by showing them a planet in broad daylight? When Venus is the evening star, carefully note where one must stand in a schoolyard to see Venus appear just on top of a nearby telephone pole or chimney, and note the time to the nearest minute. Tomorrow evening, go outside exactly an hour earlier, stand in the same spot, and hold out a hand at arm's length with the thumb at the same pole or chimney and little finger straight up—Venus should appear near the tip of the little finger. Now, walk to a new position in the schoolyard to make Venus appear on top of the same landmark once again. Repeat this exercise each afternoon an hour earlier. In less than a week, just by knowing where to stand and look, Venus will be readily seen at high noon, a feat sure to impress friends and teachers!

From lower left to upper right, the Moon,
Venus, and Jupiter glitter over the city lights
of Phoenix, Arizona.

Further Information

Beatty, J. Kelly, Carolyn Collins Petersen, and Andrew
     Chaikin (editors), *The New Solar System* (fourth
     edition, Sky Publishing Co. and Cambridge
     University Press, 1999).

Gupta, Rajiv, *Observer's Handbook*, The Royal
     Astronomical Society of Canada, (University of
     Toronto Press, published annually).

Hartmann, William K., "Mysteries of Mars," *Sky &
     Telescope*, vol. 106, no. 1, pp. 36–43 (July 2003).

Lubick, Naomi, "Goldilocks and the three planets,"
     Astronomy, vol. 31, no. 7, pp. 36–41 (July
     2003).

Thomas, Peter, "Mysteries of the Martian poles,"
     Astronomy, vol. 31, no. 3, pp. 48–53 (March
     2003).

Home page for "The Nine Planets: A Multimedia To
     the Solar System"
     http://seds.lpl.arizona.edu/nineplanets/ninepl
     ets/nineplanets.html

Views of the Solar System photo archive index page
     Mercury, Venus, Earth, and Mars
     http://www.solarviews.com/cap/index

Glossary

caldera—The crater in a volcano from which lava flows.

core—The center, or middle. A planet's core is frequently hotter than its surface and is under great pressure.

crust—The surface of a planet or moon where rock and mineral comes in contact with an atmosphere or ocean.

day, sidereal—The length of time required for a planet to rotate once on its axis and face the same stars; may radically differ from the planet's solar day.

day, solar—The length of time required for a planet to rotate once on its axis and face the Sun (e.g., from sunrise to sunrise or from one local noon to the next local noon); may radically differ from the planet's sidereal day.

eclipse—An astronomical event when one object either totally or partially blocks the view of another object.

escarpment or scarp—A long, high wall or cliff.

gravity—A force associated with bodies in motion when a rotating object creates a force of attraction.

greenhouse effect—Temperature rise on a planet's surface due to its atmosphere's absorption of ultraviolet and visible radiation and trapping of infrared (heat) radiation.

magma—Liquid rock beneath the crust of a planet that erupts at the surface as volcanic lava.

mantle—Thick layer of hot, liquid rock beneath a planet's crust, on which the crust floats.

mare—Flat, volcanic plains on the moon that ancient astronomers thought were seas (*mare* is Latin singular for "sea"; plural is *maria*).

planitia—Flat plains on Mercury, similar to *maria* on the moon.

regolith—Thin outer layer of dust coating the crust of the Moon and other solar system bodies.

revolution—One complete journey around a body that is outside an object and serves as an axis. One revolution of Earth around the Sun is a year.

shield volcano—A type of volcano so named because it is gently curved like a medieval shield, broad compared to its height; shield volcanoes are found on Venus, Earth, and Mars.

Index

48

Peabody Public Library
Columbia City, IN